Ever
PTS

Gloria C. Mathiesen
MA, LMT, NCTMB

Every Superhero has a Kryptonite:
PTSD and the Massage Therapist

Copyright © 2013
By: Gloria C. Mathiesen MA, LMT, NCTMB

All Rights Reserved. No part of this book may be reproduced or transmitted in any form or by any means, including photocopying, recording, or by any information storage and retrieval system without prior written permission of the Publisher.

Book Design: Gloria C. Mathiesen
Editor: Gloria C. Mathiesen

ISBN: 978-1480062580

First Printing: 2013

This book is dedicated to all the military families that I've met during my stay in El Paso. It has been an honor to serve you and much gratitude towards all that you do for us.

Table of Contents

Chapter 1: El Paso   7

Chapter 2: Post-Traumatic Stress Disorder   15

Chapter 3: What our role is as a Massage Therapist and Body worker:
           Treating the Symptoms of PTSD.   27

Chapter 4: Contraindications and Concerns of PTSD   47

References   57

Reiki Training   59

Chapter 1
El Paso

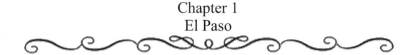

When I relocated to El Paso during the summer of 2011, I had no idea the impact it would have on my massage career of then almost 15 years. Not too long before I arrived, the city's army base (Fort Bliss) had inherited thousands of military families that I would soon have the pleasure of serving. Little did I realize – I was to be enlightened about a very special population. A population that I live amongst, socialize with, work with, and have been providing massage therapy for entire families. Some were waiting to be deployed once again, others recently coming back from a long tour. Whatever the case may have been, for those 60 minutes, my focus was always the same. To facilitate as much healing as possible.

Not all of my clients are military – yet I owe much of my success to them. Considering that my business location is on the other side of town from Fort Bliss, it still amazes me that about 60% of my clientele are military. They have interwoven themselves to where everyone is connected to some extent. I think it's important to remember you need something to connect to.

Maybe it is because the heart of El Paso feels connected. Most of the community who were born and raised in El Paso – stay in El Paso – which is a good chunk of the population. The military has brought much financial stability to the city and a sense of security. Economical stability and safety, El Paso ranks high, and appears to only be continuing in a positive direction. It was one of the main drives that brought me here.

I come from an auto union upbringing. Born and raised in the outskirts of Detroit, my father worked his entire life at the Ford Motor Transmission Plant in Livonia, Michigan. My grandfathers served for the military on both sides of the family, but my exposure has been pretty limited until I moved out west. Before El Paso, I lived in Oro Valley, Arizona, a northern suburb of Tucson where the Davis-Monthan Air force Base is located. It was a very different experience – almost like two worlds. You had the air force down south, while the rest of us – a mix of transient, seasonal, locals, students, and touristy populations were central and north. We all knew the base was south of us, but it never felt like the worlds were connected. At least to me it didn't.

Besides the military, I've found the PTSD diagnosis in other clients as well, where I wouldn't normally expect it. Traumatic car accidents seem to be the second leading cause of PTSD diagnosis for me. Perhaps it is because I am assisting them with residual physical trauma and injury. For massage therapists, the odds will probably run high with our encounter of PTSD if there was a physical trauma attached. Your client will not be coming to you specifically for PTSD – rather rehabilitation for whip lash, chronic pain, and anxiety/insomnia. Their doctor may have even recommended massage simply to relax. Whatever the case may be, we need to stay open to all root causes, and never assume where or how PTSD may come through our doors. Don't assume just because a client has written military under employment on their intake form that they automatically have PTSD. This holds the same for a client who is seeking pain relief because of a recent car accident. I am simply sharing what clients I have seen PTSD surface and it was usually shared later on in treatment as a "By the way…".

I think it is safe to assume at some point in our careers we will come across PTSD indirectly during extensive treatment plans and it is important to understand it and how we can directly assist with the healing process. I think most importantly, is remembering our scope of practice. We work with the body. We effect the tissues and all the body systems that work together to maintain homeostasis. We are not mental health counselors and absolutely under no circumstance should we ever take on that role. Even if you are a mental health counselor, if you are providing massage therapy in that moment, it is important to maintain your boundaries and provide the services in which your client has hired and paid you for. If you are working as a massage therapist, you are only covered under your liability insurance for the massage services you are providing, not for mental health counseling. One step out of that scope of practice puts your career at risk and the best interests of your client at risk.

I often feel like a broken record in several of my writings about the issues of working within our scope of practice. But I feel it wouldn't be thorough of me if I didn't bring it up with this special population. People who have been diagnosed with PTSD are a special population because they may require special accommodations during treatment. They may need shorter time sessions, quiet environment, side-line bolstering, whatever the case may be – it is important to understand their needs. It is just important for us to understand what we can accommodate and what we need to refer to another professional.

Massage therapy and other types of body work are never cure-alls. With PTSD, massage therapy and body work should never be utilized as the sole treatment. Your client should be under the care of a licensed medical or mental health professional – hopefully the person who originally made the diagnosis. Remember, our focus will always be the symptoms associated with PTSD. We are not trained, licensed, or covered by liability insurance to provide treatment plans for PTSD or any other diagnosable mental disorder.

In the next few chapters we will look at what PTSD actually is and how as massage and bodywork practitioners we can help facilitate their healing by working directly with the body and the autonomic nervous system. I hope you find this information useful and you are able to help an unfortunate growing population who can benefit greatly from the therapy that you uniquely provide.

Chapter 2
Post-Traumatic Stress Disorder

In 2000, the APA (American Psychiatric Association), revised the PTSD diagnostic criteria in the fourth edition of its Diagnostic and Statistical Manual of Mental Disorders (DSM-IV-TR) (1). The diagnostic criteria (A-F) are specified below.

Diagnostic criteria for PTSD include a history of exposure to a traumatic event meeting two criteria and symptoms from each of three symptom clusters: intrusive recollections, avoidant/numbing symptoms, and hyper-arousal symptoms. A fifth criterion concerns duration of symptoms and a sixth assesses functioning.

Criterion A: stressor

The person has been exposed to a traumatic event in which both of the following have been present:

1. The person has experienced, witnessed, or been confronted with an event or events that involve actual or threatened death or serious injury, or a threat to the physical integrity of oneself or others.

2. The person's response involved intense fear, helplessness, or horror. Note: in children, it may be expressed instead by disorganized or agitated behavior.

Criterion B: intrusive recollection

The traumatic event is persistently re-experienced in at least **one** of the following ways:

1. Recurrent and intrusive distressing recollections of the event, including images, thoughts, or perceptions. Note: in young children, repetitive play may occur in which themes or aspects of the trauma are expressed.

2. Recurrent distressing dreams of the event. Note: in children, there may be frightening dreams without recognizable content

3. Acting or feeling as if the traumatic event were recurring (includes a sense of reliving the experience, illusions, hallucinations, and dissociative flashback episodes, including those that occur upon awakening or when intoxicated). Note: in children, trauma-specific reenactment may occur.

4. Intense psychological distress at exposure to internal or external cues that symbolize or resemble an aspect of the traumatic event.

5. Physiologic reactivity upon exposure to internal or external cues that symbolize or resemble an aspect of the traumatic event

Criterion C: avoidant/numbing

Persistent avoidance of stimuli associated with the trauma and numbing of general responsiveness (not present before the trauma), as indicated by at least **three** of the following:

1. Efforts to avoid thoughts, feelings, or conversations associated with the trauma

2. Efforts to avoid activities, places, or people that arouse recollections of the trauma

3. Inability to recall an important aspect of the trauma

4. Markedly diminished interest or participation in significant activities

5. Feeling of detachment or estrangement from others

6. Restricted range of affect (e.g., unable to have loving feelings)

7. Sense of foreshortened future (e.g., does not expect to have a career, marriage, children, or a normal life span)

Criterion D: hyper-arousal

Persistent symptoms of increasing arousal (not present before the trauma), indicated by at least **two** of the following:

1. Difficulty falling or staying asleep
2. Irritability or outbursts of anger
3. Difficulty concentrating
4. Hyper-vigilance
5. Exaggerated startle response

Criterion E: duration

Duration of the disturbance (symptoms in B, C, and D) is more than one month.

Criterion F: functional significance

The disturbance causes clinically significant distress or impairment in social, occupational, or other important areas of functioning.

Specify if:

Acute: if duration of symptoms is less than three months

Chronic: if duration of symptoms is three months or more

Specify if:

With or Without delay onset: Onset of symptoms at least six months after the stressor (American Psychiatric Association, 2000).

If you have a client who has officially been diagnosed with PTSD from a mental health worker that means they have met the above criteria. Absolutely under no circumstances have I shared this diagnostic information for you to diagnose your client – regardless of how sure you feel your client has PTSD. First, under no circumstances are massage therapists and body workers ever under jurisdiction to diagnose anything. Doing so can put your practice at risk and held liable in a court of law. This includes all mental health disorders that may fall under the criteria of the DSM-IV-TR. To diagnose *anything* requires specific training in that field of pathology. Leave it to the experts. If you have concerns that your client *may* be symptomatic of anything – refer them out to an expert in that field. Be sure that you do not *suggest a diagnosis* – rather you feel your treatment plan is limited to their needs and this practitioner may be more appropriate.

All clinical diagnosis aside – it is important to understand PTSD in laymen terms and how massage and bodywork can have a positive effect as an adjunct to professional counseling. To simplify here are my understandings of what PTSD is and is not.

PTSD is not:

- Something to be afraid of as a practitioner.

- A crazy, out-of control lunatic.

- Contagious.

- Guaranteed flashbacks during a session.

- Associated with all military professionals.

PTSD can be:

- Something scary for the person diagnosed at times.

- Associated with shame.

- Thought of as a sign of weakness.

- A secret.

- Isolating and feeling misunderstood.

- In company with Depression, Substance abuse, and TBI (Traumatic Brain Injury).

PTSD is:

- Treatable.

- An anxiety disorder.

- Commonly associated with symptoms such as; headaches, insomnia, gastrointestinal disorders, feelings of grief and loss, feeling emotionally numb/dead, irritability, difficulty concentrating, angry outbursts, easily startled, hyper vigilant, nightmares, and flashbacks.

As massage therapists and body workers we need to take note most importantly to the following physical symptoms; pounding heart, rapid breathing, nausea, muscle tension, and sweating which are all directly linked to the sympathetic nervous system.

As massage therapists and body workers it is most important to remember and keep the main focus on the PTSD *symptoms* – not the PTSD itself. **We are treating the symptoms – not PTSD directly.**

If you were to separate the above symptoms from the PTSD, you can see how we already have several clients who claim the same upon intake. Concerns like insomnia, muscle tension, headaches, and gastrointestinal disorders are quite common and will often present themselves during an intake interview for massage therapy.

Two variables that have been studied in the massage field, state anxiety and trait anxiety, have demonstrated significant improvement from the recipient of massage and bodywork:

State anxiety is a momentary emotional reaction consisting of apprehension, tension, worry, and heightened ANS activity. Because state anxiety can be understood as a reaction to one's condition or environment, the intensity and duration of such a state is determined by an individual's perception of a situation as threatening. Many of the samples used in MT research are drawn from populations experiencing serious and chronic health problems that can lead to feelings of anxiety. If MT is effective in reducing state anxiety, it may be doubly valuable to such patient populations, in that it could both improve subjective well-being and promote physical health. In physically healthy populations, the improvement in subjective well-being alone may be the primary benefit of a reduction in state anxiety. Several studies have examined MT's potential to reduce trait anxiety, the "relatively stable individual differences in anxiety proneness as a personality trait". In contrast with the transient and situation-specific nature of state anxiety, trait anxiety is a dispositional, internalized proneness to be anxious. Persons with high levels of trait anxiety tend to perceive the world as more dangerous or threatening, and experience anxiety states more frequently and with greater intensity than those with lower levels of trait anxiety (Moyer, Rounds, and Hannum, 2004).

What is most important for the massage therapist and body worker to understand is what PTSD is and what symptoms may surface during treatment and how to deal with them. Also, last but not least, how to make your treatment room and experience as comfortable as possible for an individual who has been diagnosed with PTSD.

In the next chapter we will discuss exactly what our role is in this journey of the client and how we can be effective in helping alleviate the symptoms that may be present.

Massage and PTSD

"In one study, massage therapy was found to decrease anxiety, depression, and cortisol levels in children who survived Hurricane Andrew. Children received 30 minutes of back massage per session, twice per week, for 8 days over a one-month period. The children's self-drawings were also analyzed and indicated lower problem scores on their last day drawings than their first-day drawings."

Field T et al: Alleviating posttraumatic stress in children following Hurricane Andrew, J Appl Dev Psychol 17:37-50, 1996.

Chapter 3
What our role is as a Massage Therapist and Body worker: Treating the Symptoms of PTSD.

Massage therapy has been repeatedly defined as a manual manipulation of soft tissue intended to promote health and well-being. Historically, the benefits of massage have been recorded as far back as 2000 B.C. The Chinese, Egyptians, Greeks, Hindus, Japanese, and Romans considered it part of their medical practice. Massage's therapeutic effects have been directly connected with touch and rubbing – contact with the skin. Recent research suggests we effect by other means as well. During my research I came across incredible data that offered a psychotherapy perspective of massage therapy:

Another theory that has not previously been put forth may also account for MT effects. MT may provide benefit in a way that parallels the common-factors model of psychotherapy. Substantial evidence suggests that the considerable efficaciousness of psychotherapy results not from any specific ingredient of treatment, but rather from the factors that all forms of psychotherapy share (Wampold, 2001). In this model, factors such as a client who has positive expectations for treatment, a therapist who is warm and has positive regard for the client, and the development of an alliance between the therapist and client are considered to be more important than adherence to a specific modality of psychotherapy. The same model can be extended to MT, given the possibility that benefits arising from it may come about more from factors such as the recipient's attitude toward MT, the therapist's personal characteristics and expectations, and the interpersonal contact and communication that take place during treatment, as opposed to the specific form of MT used or the site to which it is applied.

Several of the findings in the present study are consistent with such a model applied to MT. The finding that MT has an effect on trait anxiety and depression that is similar in magnitude to what would be expected to result from psychotherapy suggests the possibility that these different treatments may be more similar than previously considered. Further support comes from the fact that MT training was not predictive of effects. Possibly, MT effects are more closely linked with characteristics of the massage provider that are independent of skill or experience in performing soft tissue manipulation.

In addition to having similar effects, MT parallels psychotherapy in structure. Both forms of therapy routinely rely on repeated, private interpersonal contact between two persons. Studies contributing effects to the trait anxiety and depression outcome categories used treatment protocols similar to those that might be maintained in short-term psychotherapy, with twice-weekly meetings over a span of 5 weeks being most common; other studies used similar protocols. Interestingly, the length of individual sessions in these studies ranged from 15 to 40 min, with 30 min being the most common session length. Had these studies used a session length equivalent to the "50-minute hour" that is routine in psychotherapy, it is possible that MT's effect for these variables would have matched or exceeded that expected of psychotherapy.

Application of such a psychotherapeutic, common-factors model to MT has important ramifications for future research. Different questions need to be asked, different moderators tested, and different comparisons made. Foremost among the questions is whether MT is as effective as psychotherapy. No study has directly compared these treatments, a comparison that would be justified given the finding that some MT effects may be very similar to those of psychotherapy. Similarly, it could be interesting to determine whether a combination of MT and psychotherapy could be significantly more effective than either alone. Another critical issue that needs to be examined is whether these specific MT effects are enduring. Current studies contributing to these effects all performed assessments on the final day of treatment, making it impossible to know if the effects last. Studies that administer a course of MT treatment should make assessments not only immediately after treatment has ended, but also several weeks or months later, to determine whether reductions of anxiety, depression, or other conditions are maintained.

Despite the fact that MT is a treatment that relies on interpersonal contact, no research has attempted to manipulate, or even measure, the kind of psychological interactions that undoubtedly take place between the provider and recipient of MT. Details worth examining include (a) the amount and types of communication, both verbal and nonverbal, that take place between massage therapist and recipient; (b) the recipient's and therapist's expectations for whether treatment will be beneficial; (c) the amount of empathy perceived by the recipient on behalf of the therapist; (d) whether the psychological state of the therapist is of importance; and (e) whether personality traits of the therapist, of the recipient, or any interaction between those personality traits influence outcomes. An examination of such personality, process, and therapeutic relationship variables may reveal that benefiting from MT is just as much about feeling valued as it is about being kneaded.

Finally, the possibility that MT may provide a significant portion of its benefit in a way that parallels psychotherapy has a bearing on the selection of comparison treatments used in future research. Viewed from a medical perspective, comparison treatments in MT research are thought to function as placebo treatments, in that they control for incidental aspects of the treatment (most notably attention in MT research) while withholding what is thought to be the specific effective ingredient (soft tissue manipulation). However, the same logic cannot be applied if the treatment being examined is thought to be beneficial because of incidental aspects, because the double-blind condition favored in medicine trials, where neither the participants nor the researchers involved in the study are aware of who is receiving viable treatment and who is receiving the placebo, is logically impossible (Wampold, 2001, p. 129). Those supervising and administering treatment in MT research, as in psychotherapy research, are aware of the treatment being delivered and know if it is intended to be therapeutic. This is a critical factor to consider if the treatment being studied relies on the therapist's beliefs and intentions in order to be effective. The placebo treatment, derived from medical trials intended to examine the effectiveness of specific ingredients, cannot control for the incidental aspects of a treatment such as MT. When a common-factors model is applied to MT, the notion that a comparison treatment such as progressive muscle relaxation controls for attention is incorrect. The attention provided to comparison group participants is identical in quantity but not in quality, and cannot be expected to function as a control for the attention received by participants in the MT treatment group.

The idea that MT has significant parallels with psychotherapy, and that perspectives gained from psychotherapeutic research should be applied to future research, is not meant to suggest that MT delivers effects entirely by psychological means. Clearly MT is at least partially a physical therapy, and some of its benefits almost certainly occur through physiological mechanisms. In fact, one of the most interesting aspects of MT is that it may deliver benefit in multiple ways; specific ingredients and common factors may each play a role, with each being differentially important depending on the desired effect. However, whether researchers wish to study MT as a physical therapy, as a psychological one, or as both, new research should examine not merely the effects resulting from MT, but also the ways in which these effects come about. It is only by testing MT theories that a better understanding of this ancient practice will result (Moyer, Rounds, and Hannum, 2004).

This perspective does not suggest using massage therapy as an alternative to psychotherapy. On the contrary, it suggests that when the two are used in combination, the positive effects of both may be increased.

In addition, further research has taken place working specifically with the military population suffering from PTSD. By adding massage to therapy, treatment becomes more effective and there is less stigma of weakness associated with psychotherapy used alone:

Post-traumatic stress disorder (PTSD) is a common and persistent problem in military populations that warrants swift and effective treatment. Recent estimates suggest that among recent Iraq and Afghanistan veterans, 21.8% are diagnosed with PTSD, with prevalence rates increasing 4 to 7 times after the invasion of Iraq. Substance use disorders, depression, and interpersonal conflicts also substantially increase in these soldiers and physical health-related consequences such as increased risk for hypertension and diabetes have also been noted. Not surprisingly, the incidence of PTSD appears to increase with combat exposure.

Despite all best efforts to treat PTSD in our military, it remains untreated in a substantial number of those on active duty and/or recently deployed. These soldiers are more likely to report mental health issues compared to their reserve comrades, and yet are significantly less likely to engage in mental health services. In general, the younger cohort of Operations Enduring Freedom/Iraqi Freedom veterans are notably loathe to seek conventional PTSD treatment, in part, because of perceived stigmatization and negative beliefs about conventional mental health care (i.e., psychotherapy and medications). Even for those who may be open to seeking treatment, data suggests there are large numbers of military personnel who may not meet clinical cutoffs for PTSD immediately upon return from deployment, but whose symptoms escalate to clinical levels even up to 12 months post deployment. These findings suggest a need for swift, effective, and no stigmatizing treatment of PTSD symptoms in post deployment active duty personnel, as well as speak to the need to address PTSD symptoms for active duty military in general health care settings as opposed to providing PTSD treatment solely in mental health care settings. Similar to civilian populations, complementary and alternative medicine (CAM) approaches are often sought out by military personnel, for a variety of health conditions. Recent studies estimate CAM use in U.S. Military populations to range between 39.3 and 50.7%. The largest epidemiological study reported that 41% of military personnel had reported CAM use in the past year, with 27% reporting use of practitioner-assisted CAM therapies (such as acupuncture, biofeedback, and bio-field/energy healing). Interestingly, the study reported that use of CAM was nearly doubled compared to no CAM use for those with a PTSD diagnosis, suggesting that military personnel with PTSD are relatively high users of CAM (Jain, S., McMahon, G. F.,N.C.U.S.N., Hasen, P., Kozub, M. P.,N.C.U.S.N., Porter, V., King, R., & Guarneri, E. M., M.D., 2012).

    This shift is happening. A more holistic approach is being offered to this special population diagnosed with PTSD and is meeting the upswing demand. The question is; how do we as massage and body workers gage our role in an ethical manner? What are our parameters and how does this population fit in our scope of practice? To simplify the answer, we go all the way back to our anatomy and physiology classes offered in our massage program, and recall the lecture on the central nervous system. More specifically how massage directly affects our central nervous system. By keeping our focus and intent of this therapeutic benefit of massage, we will always remain in our scope of practice.

Stress, in this case post-traumatic stress, has a direct effect on the central nervous system along with other body systems.

Psychological stress has numerous physiologic, metabolic, and behavioral consequences. All of these are triggered when a particular situation is perceived as stressful. A prominent stress theory postulates that this perception is associated with the appraisal of the situation; when the demands of the particular even are perceived to exceed the available resources, the feeling of stress ensues. However, besides the appraisal, there are specific situational circumstances that contribute to stress perception. A thorough meta-analysis of a little more than 200 human studies of psychological stress induction revealed that situational characteristics facilitating the generation of a stress response include an atmosphere of high achievement, social evaluation, and little or no controllability. This finding supports the social self-preservation theory, which posits that humans have a strong need to preserve their social self (one's social values, esteem, and status), and are vigilant to threats that may jeopardize this identity. Interestingly, in neuroimaging studies, the network that has been associated with self-referential thought is similar to the network of structures observed is association with the phenomenon of psychological stress.

Psychological stress is a potent trigger of the most important neuroendocrine stress system in animals and humans, the HPA axis. In response to perceived stress, the hypothalamus release CRF, which induces secretion of ACTH from the pituitary. Circulating ACTH targets the adrenal cortex and induces synthesis and secretion of glucocorticoids (cortisol in humans, corticosterone in rats) from the adrenal cortex. Released glucocorticoids exert their effects on several target systems throughout the organism, including the central nervous , metabolic, immune, and cardiovascular systems, all with an aim to increase the availability of energy substrates and to allow optimal adaptation to heightened demands from the environment. Moreover, glucocorticoids impact on subsequent HPA axis activation via negative feedback exerted on the axis at the level of pituitary and hypothalamus. An additional regulatory network is formed by structures that are also high in glucocorticoid receptors, namely, hippocampus, PFC, and amygdala

(Dedovic, K., D'Aguiar, C., & Pruessner, J. C., PhD, 2009).

I am going to do a brief review of anatomy and physiology – specifically with our autonomic nervous system (ANS). Within our ANS we have two divisions; the sympathetic nervous system (SNS) and the parasympathetic nervous system (PNS). The nickname for our PNS is the rest-and-digest division. This division dominates during rest and supports the body functions that conserve and restore body energy, such as the digestive system. The PNS is most active during calm situations and will stimulate visceral organs for normal functions as it maintains homeostasis. Other body processes associated with our PNS are salivation, urination, digestive processes, defecation, and storing nutrients to use later as needed. During a massage or other relaxing body work modalities, the parasympathetic is responding, which helps broaden your client's perceptual field. One gift we give our clients during massage and bodywork is a relaxed state of mind in which he or she may contemplate additional options and/or solutions to life's challenges.

When a stressful situation arises, the sympathetic system, nicknamed as our fight-or-flight division, takes over. It will override the parasympathetic during physical exertion or emotional stress.

The sympathetic response requires body energy. When we've switched over to fight-or-flight mode our pupils will dilate, our heart rate increases, our blood pressure rises, we will have a dilation of our airways and a constriction of blood vessels in our digestive tract. This shuts off digestion and allows more blood to circulate to our skeletal muscles and heart. These reactions occur within seconds.

Without our sympathetic nervous system we would never get out of bed. We would have no motivation to do anything. The problem comes when we exist primarily in chronic state of stress or primarily in our sympathetic nervous system. Eventually glands do burn out, like our adrenals, and lead to chronic disease. Stress can be linked to just about all chronic illnesses and the sad thing is that it can be managed. In this case with PTSD, the client is stuck in an extreme hyper response to physical and psychological stress. The way we can effect clients diagnosed with PTSD is how massage impacts the autonomic nervous system. Massage essentially shuts off the sympathetic and turns on the parasympathetic. Within minutes! The power of touch can combat chronic, pathological stress with good intentions and focus. A proper treatment plan is a must when the goal is stress management and using appropriate modalities are crucial. Sticking to modalities such as Swedish, Trager, Therapeutic Touch, and Reiki are a few in which client's diagnosed with PTSD would benefit highly from.

Reiki

Recently, I had the pleasure of taking a Reiki I course with a friend and colleague here in El Paso, Keith Roseman, who owns the Southwest Wellness Clinic. I intend on completing the training for master's and teacher's level to further my understanding of energy work and how to integrate it into my practice.

I had always heard about chakras, Chi, Auras, gem stones, and knew a little about essential oils – but never really understood enough to speak intelligently about any of it. During the class, it hit me, this modality would be perfect for PTSD! Especially for those who are so sensitive to external stimuli, since Reiki doesn't even require the practitioner to apply any physical contact.

I'm not even going to attempt to write about Reiki as I'm just learning. If you are in or near the city of El Paso, Texas, I highly recommend you to take Keith's class. If you are in or near the Greater Milwaukee area, I highly recommend two dear friends of mine, Jan Soldon-Nelan and Rev. Kenneth J. Nelan.

"The main chakras to focus on are heart, throat, solar plexus, and root. The person needs ground, but must do so through releasing the stressors which built up over time - even if only a short time. The throat chakra to help release, the solar plexus to help refill and stabilize, the root to ground and help bring back to center - and the heart - the heart is the way all healing is tempered and someone suffering PTSD must take care to feel "slowly" and must take special care to separate out the pain from the event.

Time... patience... working above the person rather than on... using common sense with Reiki and knowing when enough is enough are all important when working with someone who suffers PTSD. Someone suffering PTSD should also be encouraged to use Reiki as a complementary procedure. If one is not seeking professional psychological or psychiatric assistance, then they should be encouraged to do so - along with receiving Reiki treatments. We need to remember that Reiki is not a cure-all, though it can cure. It is a complementary modality to be used with other available medical and psychiatric procedures. And as always, if a person is heavily medicated then like with Massage, Reiki is NOT recommended due to the altered mental and physical state." (Rev. Kenneth J. Nelan).

In a beginner's nutshell, a chakra is an energy vortex which spins and draws in universal life force energy. We actually have 7 main chakras which align in an ascending column from the base of our spine to the top of our head. Each chakra is associated with several physiological, emotional, and spiritual functions.

I'm going to stop right there.

As Keith stated in class, Reiki is not voodoo, witch craft, or magic, it has been around since the early 1900's. It has even been introduced and utilized within the medical community by nurses in hospitals. The important thing to remember is that the client has to be open to receiving Reiki. Ethically speaking, always discuss every modality with your clients and ask permission to move forward with application.

I've personally received Reiki by different practitioners and it has always been a positive experience. Just like massage, each Reiki session felt unique to that practitioner, yet very beneficial. As a Reiki Practitioner, I've enjoyed providing the service for a variety of clients. It is a modality that when done appropriately, does not leave you physically exhausted like deep tissue work can. After your attunement, you are nothing more than a conduit and all that is required are good intentions towards your client's well-being.

Chapter 4
Contraindications and Concerns of PTSD

One of the best ways to approach PTSD is with prevention of the "What if..".

"What if they have a flashback during session?"

"What if they go crazy with anger?"

"What if they start crying uncontrollably and I can't help them?"

"What if I say something or do something that triggers a memory?"

Depending on how long you've been in practice, there is a very good possibility that you've already worked on a client with clinical PTSD. They may never have told because they were too ashamed, or, they haven't been diagnosed yet. People diagnosed with PTSD are the last ones you would witness running aimlessly, crazy in a panic, crying uncontrollably, and spouting out anger towards everyone around. On the contrary, people with PTSD often become very isolated and home-bound, because they are too afraid to interact with the "real world". Regardless, the last thing you want to do is approach the session with fear and "What if…". The best prevention of an incident is education and even then life happens. Creating a safe and genuine space for treatment is the best thing that you can do. Have confidence in you and your work. The more confidence you present, the less anxiety you will be putting off, and the less your client will feel apprehensive about the whole situation. This book, as small as it may be, accompanies a continuing education class for NCBTMB worth 3 credit hours. The class is geared for massage therapists and body workers, as well as, anyone working within the integrated field of modalities for health and wellness. I've travelled around as much as I can and will continue to do so, but my base is in Ann Arbor, Michigan. If my courses are not convenient for you, check out what your community offers on this topic and start learning about this population who is in great need of assistance towards health and well-being.

If this population doesn't seem like a good fit for you – it's okay – just make sure you have a reference or two to send them for treatment. As massage therapists and body workers, we are not meant to serve every single special population known to mankind. We all have limits for whatever reasons they may be. The best thing you can do – and the most ethical – is to know your limits and when to say "No".

Your Treatment Room

I think the number one requirement when working with this particular client is that your location provides privacy, peace and quiet, and your sessions will be uninterrupted. Currently, I struggle with this because my space is located within a yoga studio. The studio also holds ballet, Zumba, belly dancing, and Pilate's classes' at all different times of the day and evenings. It is a great and healthy environment to be a part of; however, when working with special populations I have to be very careful with scheduling. If you plan on working mostly with clients who have been diagnosed with PTSD – your location is going to determine as to whether your sessions will be therapeutic or not. Abrupt, loud noise can send your client into a high anxiety state of mind, which you will be responsible for calming down.

You want to project a warm, friendly, comforting environment. Soft scents if any and quiet surroundings. Be prepared to work without music or barely noticeable. Your intake and interview should be thorough, which means, make sure you've scheduled plenty of time so neither one of you feels rushed. Discuss comfortable time limits, positioning on table, and working side-line with bolsters. Some clients may feel uncomfortable lying prone staring down in the face cradle. Explain what modalities you'd like to suggest and ask permission to use each one. Make sure the client understands that at any time during session, they may change their mind and decide they no longer want to receive a certain modality. A simple hand gesture or word can be used to stop the session in progress. Taking breaks may be necessary and sessions may be cut short as needed. Emphasize the client may disrobe to their comfort level and draping will be used at all times. Heavier than usual draping may actually create a comforting and more secure feeling. Inform your client before performing any mobilizations, specifically if you will be lifting at the wrists and ankles. Stay mindful of their emotional stability and stop if you sense any anxiety. The key word is – flexible – until you and your client develop trust, you can't be certain what to expect at first.

Your Intake and Interview

Whether your client has been referred to you as an adjunct to their PTSD treatment or they simply have checked off "PTSD" on the intake form, the most important thing to ask your client is – what are their triggers? You don't need details of the incident (s) that actually caused the PTSD – *just the triggers associated with PTSD*. Most people will know at least one trigger. It could be a sound, smell, taste, color, certain body positions, or touch. Ask specifically if there are any areas of their body that would be considered contraindicated. Also, if you will be working simultaneously with your client's psychiatrist or physician, you will need to get a written consent in order to share information with the other practitioners involved. Make sure you maintain good SOAP notes and document all communication with the other practitioners.

Possible Crisis Situations during Treatment

Panic Attack.

Think intense fear. A Panic Attack will present as heart palpitations, chest pains, profuse sweating, trembling, shortness of breath, inability to speak, the walls are closing in, and there is no air, dizziness, gastrointestinal distress, chills and even hot flashes. It can look as scary as it feels, the important thing is to remain calm. If your client has a panic attack during the treatment, the best thing you can do is gently assist them into a sitting position while maintaining modesty with proper draping. Encourage your client to take slow deep breaths, counting to 4, taking the breaths with them. Make sure your movements are slow, deliberate, and quiet. Ask if you can call their emergency contact while you are in the room. Don't leave the client alone unless they ask you to leave. Most individuals will become more anxious if left by themselves. If your client mentioned that they suffer from panic attacks during your intake and interview – discuss what helps them feel balanced again. Ask what triggers are associated if any. Discussing the situation while the client feels safe and balanced may actually prevent an attack from occurring or help the intervention become more successful.

Flashback.

A flashback is essentially a memory of a past trauma. They may take on different forms such as actual scenes, sounds, smells, body sensations, feelings or lack of them (numbness). However it may transform, temporarily and completely involuntarily, your client is not presently with you. Meaning, whatever memory they are reliving, that is where your client exists. Your client will have literally "checked-out" and has become temporarily non-responsive. If your client has experienced flashbacks, it would be considered contraindicated to have them prone, facing down in a cradle. They may feel more comfortable receiving chair massage which allows them to have their feet closer to the ground. During a flashback, your client will look "spaced-out" and it is important to have a view of their facial expressions during treatment. If flashbacks are common and regular – *massage therapy would be considered contraindicated*. For this case, the trauma is most likely recent and other types of therapy and medication would be more appropriate at this time. There is such a thing as trauma being *too raw* to treat with massage therapy and body work. Sometimes it is more important to work with the mind alone first – before integrating the body.

If a client has a flashback during session, it is your job to reorient them to the present. Begin by softly but firmly calling out their name. Sometimes that alone will bring them back. When the client is coming back begin to get them grounded. Assist them off the table into a standing position, making sure to maintain modesty with draping. Communicate. Tell them your name, where they are, what day it is, why they are there – bring them back to the present. Administer the same protocol for panic attacks – as anxiety may slip in once they "return". Have them get in touch with their breathing.

Slowing our breath actually activates the parasympathetic nervous system. Suggest they place their hand on their diaphragm to feel their breath and their presence. Allow time to recover and call their emergency contact. At some point, your client may become embarrassed; it is your job to make sure you come across as supportive and understanding. Flashbacks are all part of the healing process.

I leave you with a quote from an old friend of mine. By request, their identity will remain forever anonymous. It has stayed with me and put everything in perspective.

"Flashbacks actually remind me that the trauma is over. The experience is in the past. The worst is over – only a memory left for me to deal with."

For more information on my continuing education courses you can view a complete listing at; www.continuing-ed-massage.com

References:

1. American Psychiatric Association. (2000). *Diagnostic and statistical manual of mental disorders* (Revised 4th ed.). Washington, DC: Author.

2. Slone, L.B., & Friedman, M.J. (2008). *After the War Zone: A Practical Guide for Returning Troops and Their Families* (1st ed.). Da Capo Press.

3. Simpson, C., & Simpson, D. (1997). *Coping with Post-Traumatic Stress Disorder* (1st ed.). The Rosen Publishing Group, Inc: NY.

4. Dedovic, K., D'Aguiar, C., & Pruessner, J. C., PhD. (2009). *What stress does to your brain: A review of neuroimaging studies.* Canadian Journal of Psychiatry, 54(1), 6-15.

5. Jain, S., McMahon, G. F.,N.C.U.S.N., Hasen, P., Kozub, M. P.,N.C.U.S.N., Porter, V., King, R., & Guarneri, E. M., M.D. (2012). *Healing touch with guided imagery for PTSD in returning active duty military: A randomized controlled trial.* Military Medicine, 177(9), 1015-21.

6. Salvo, S. (2007). Massage Therapy: Principles and Practice. (3rd ed.). Saunders: Elsevier.

7. Salvo, S. (2009). Mosby's Pathology for Massage Therapists. (2nd ed.). Mosby: Elsevier.

8. Moyer, C. A., Rounds, J., & Hannum, J. W. (2004). A Meta-Analysis of Massage Therapy Research. Psychological Bulletin, 130(1), 3-18.

Reiki Training:

Southwest Wellness Clinic
Owner: Gregory Keith Roseman
1848 Trawood Dr
El Paso, Texas 79935
(915) 633-6200
www.southwestwellnessclinic.com

Sacred Wandering
(Serving the Greater Milwaukee area.)
www.sacredwandering.com
414-433-9193 - No Business Solicitations!
E-mail
Reiki Masters/Teachers
•Janet C. Soldon, RM/T, LSW, MA
 Email: jsoldon@yahoo.com
•Rev. Kenneth J. Nelan, CSFD
 Email: ken.nelan@sacredwandering.com

Made in the USA
San Bernardino, CA
14 December 2014